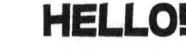

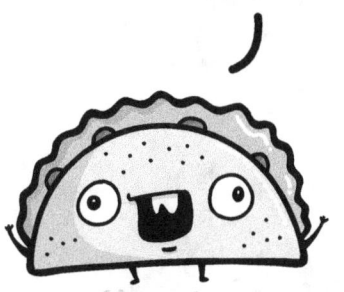

I wanted to say thanks to my
friends Mindy and Kim. Without
the both of you, this book would
still be sitting on my desk.

HOW TO DRAW
SILLY FOODS

IT'S AS EASY AS PIE!

BY DZINGEEK

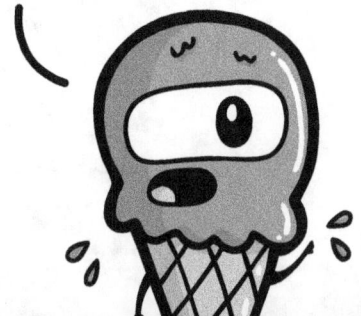

ORANGIE PEELERMAN

1.

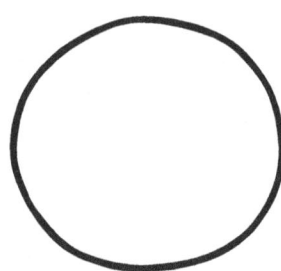

2.

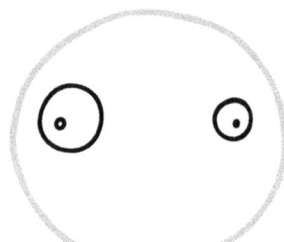

3.

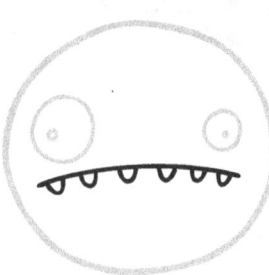

4.

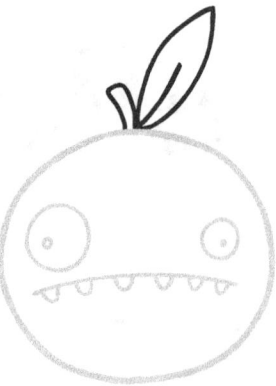

5.

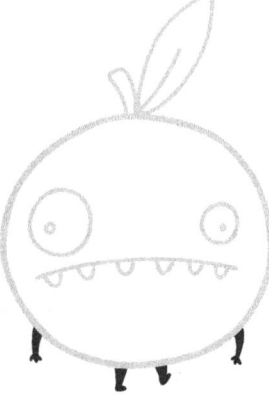

6.

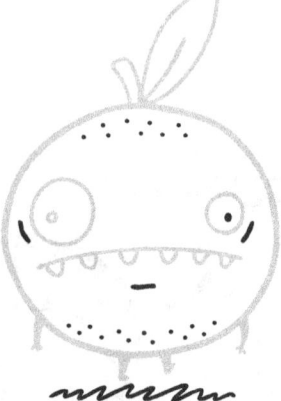

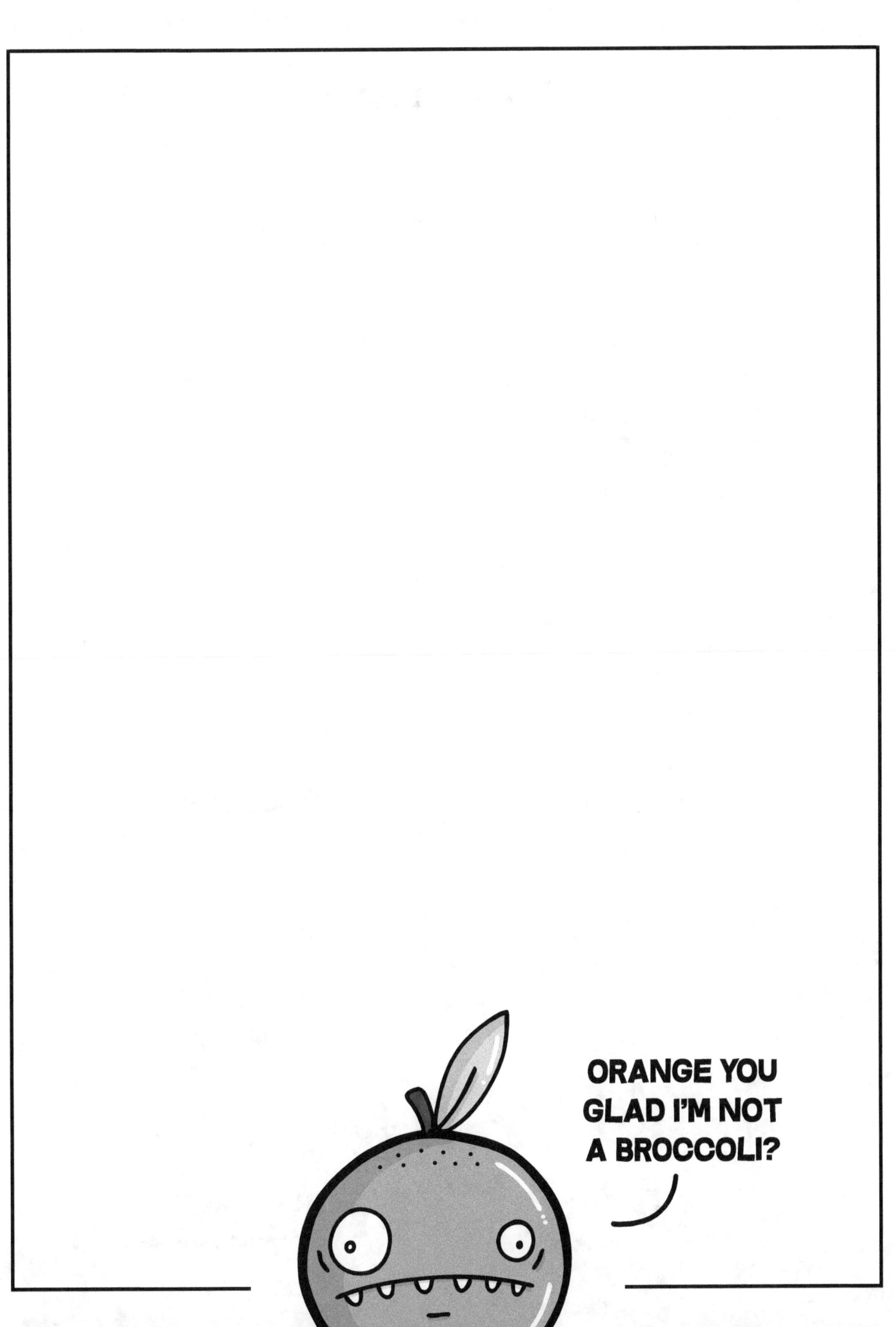

JUICY LENNY

1.

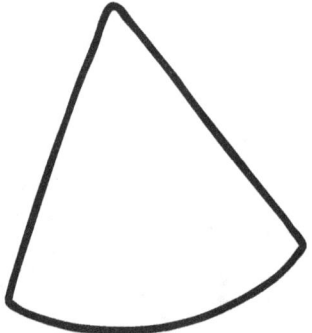

2.

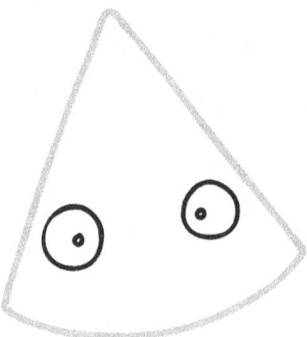

3.

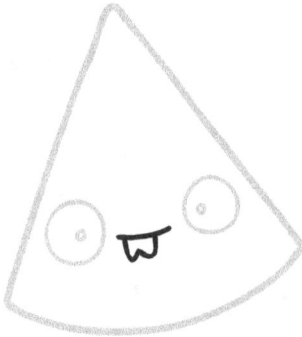

4.

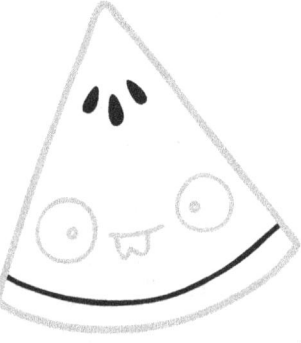

5.

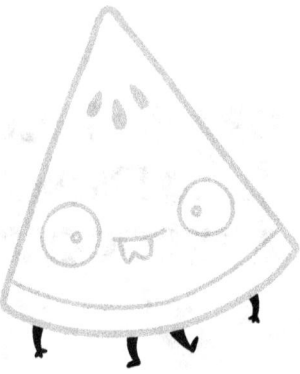

6.

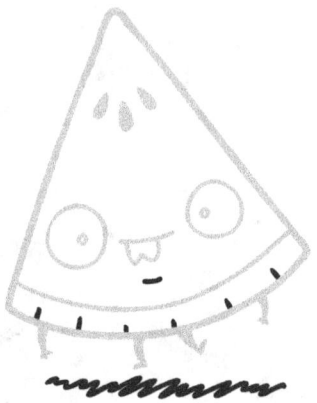

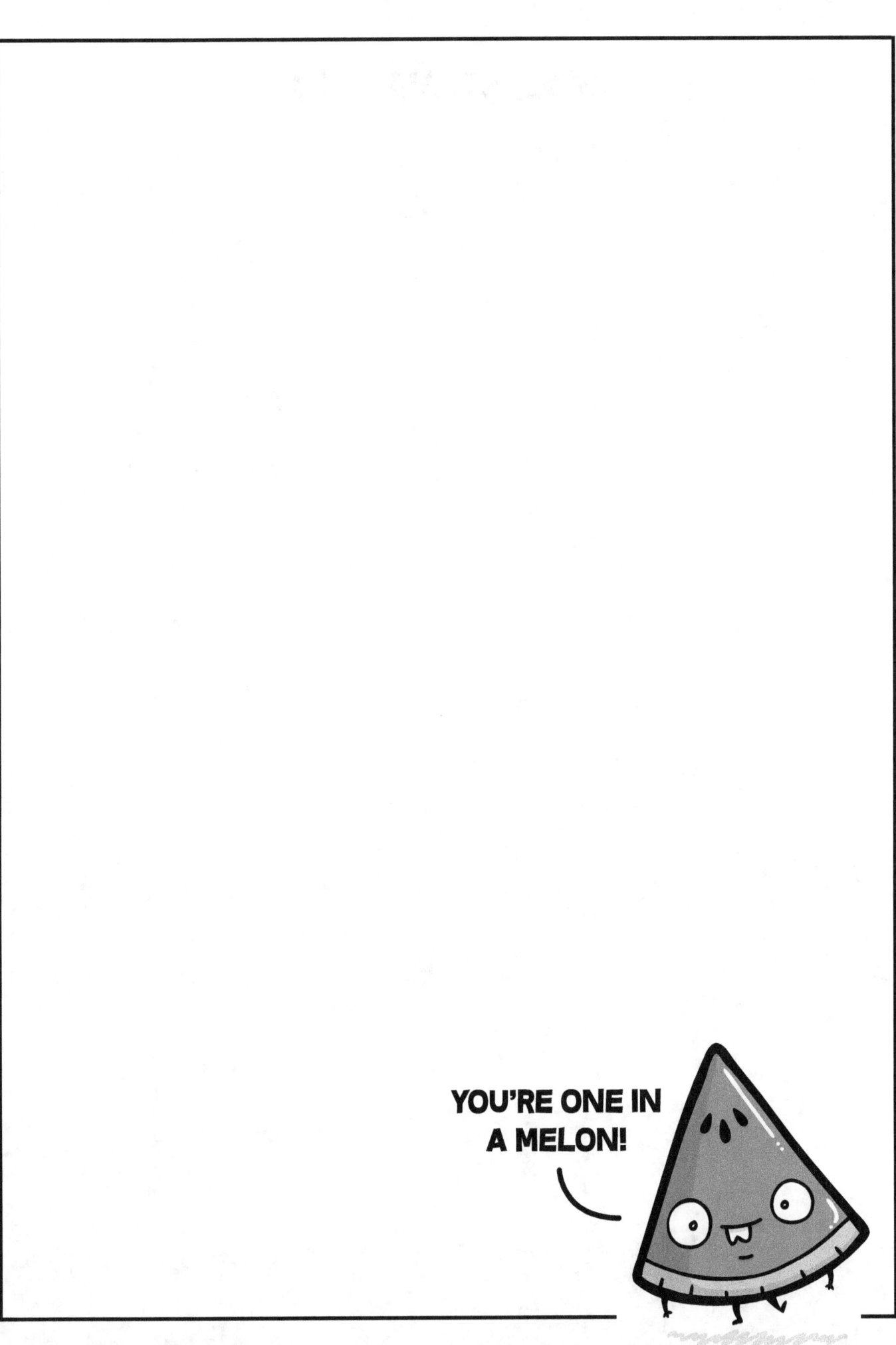

YOU'RE ONE IN A MELON!

MACHO NACHO

1.

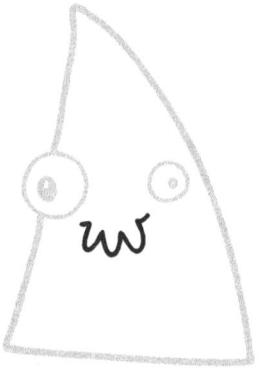

2.

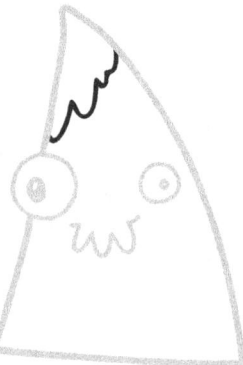

3.

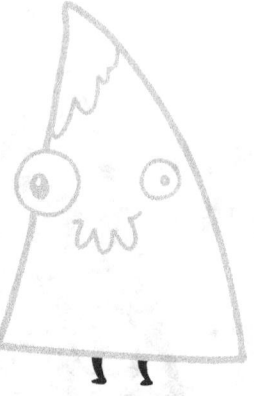

4.

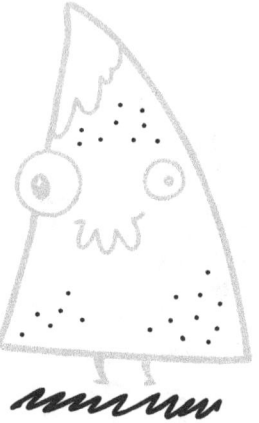

5.

6.

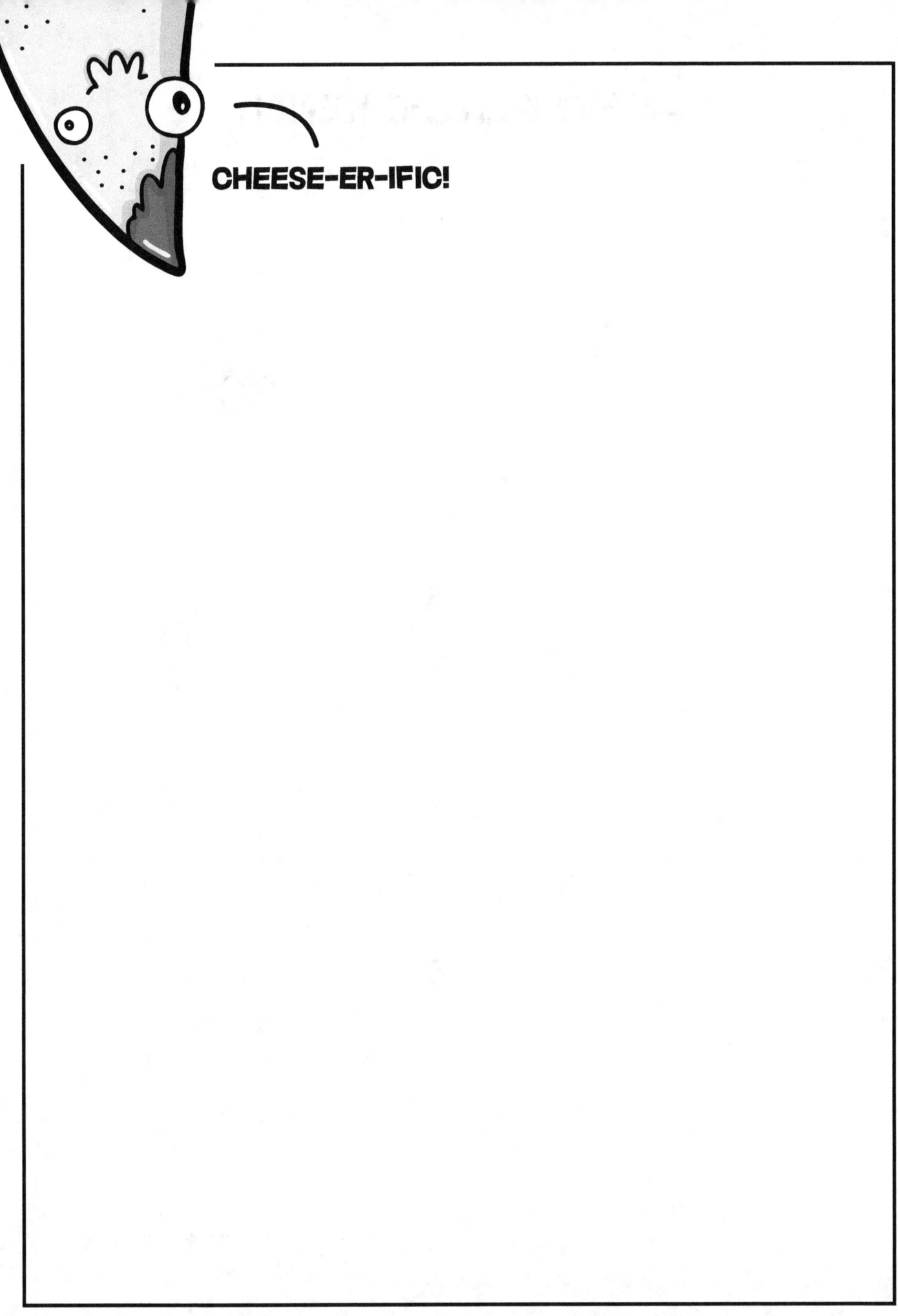

CHEESE-ER-IFIC!

ANGRY GLAZED KENNY

1.

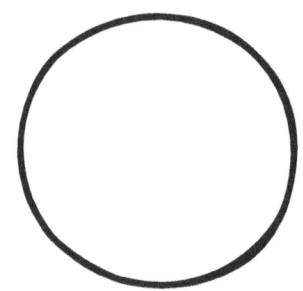

2.

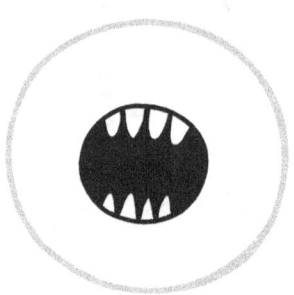

3.

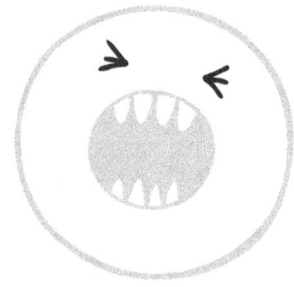

4.

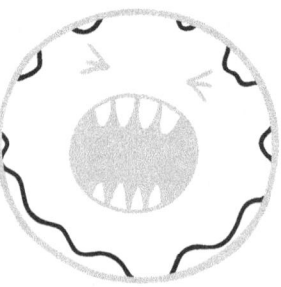

5.

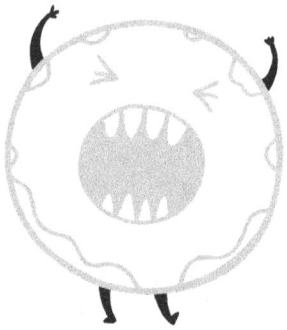

6.

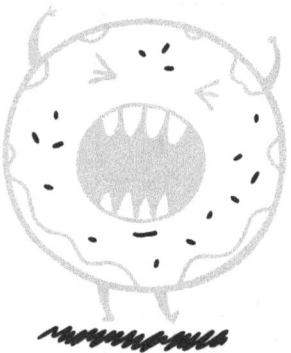

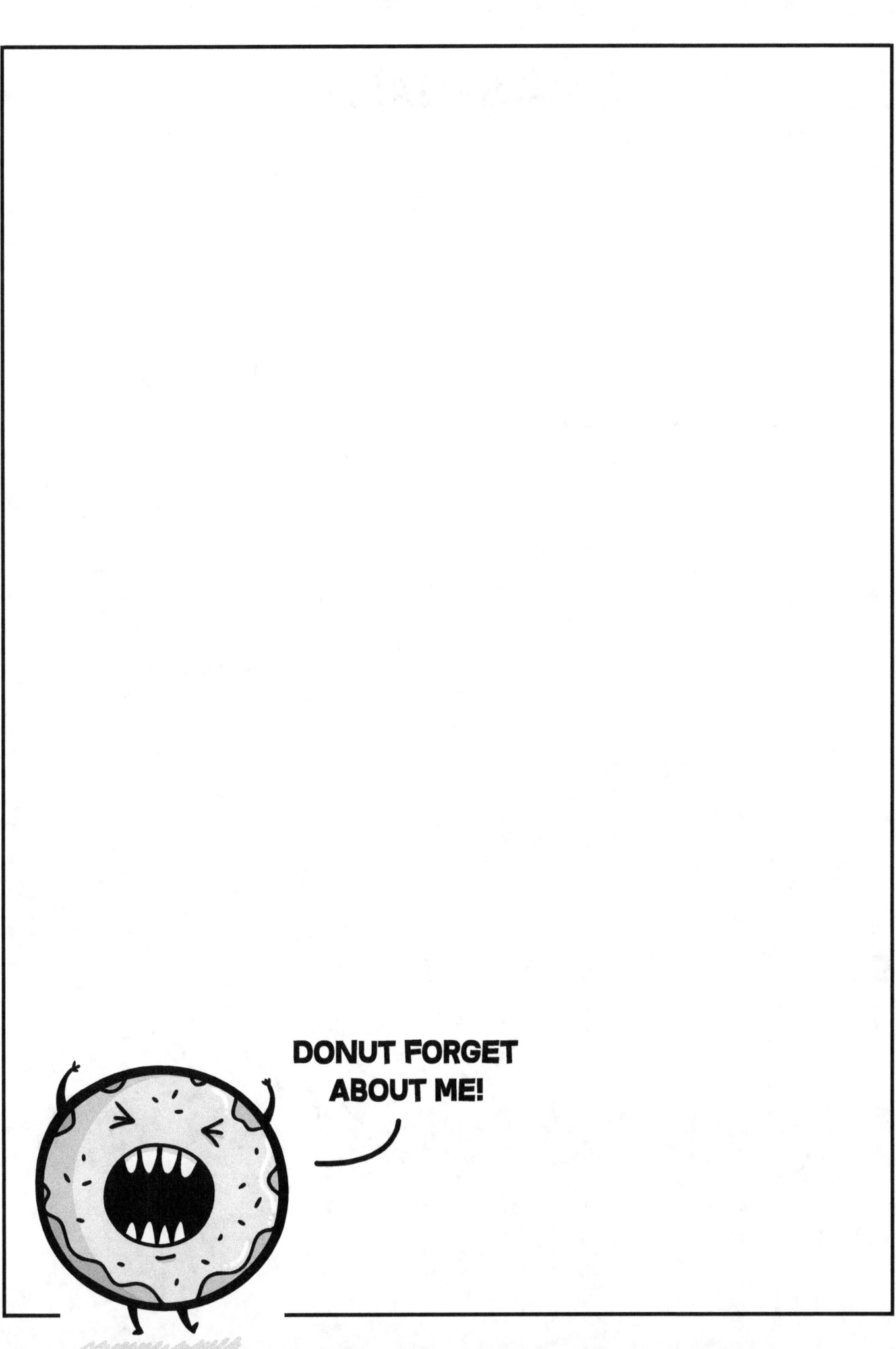

SALSA SALLY

1.

2.

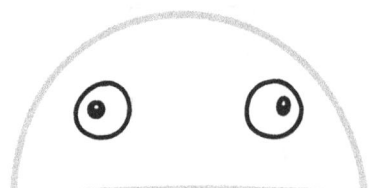

3.

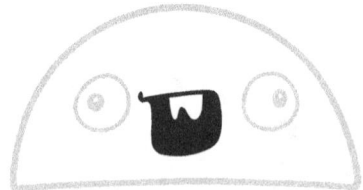

4.

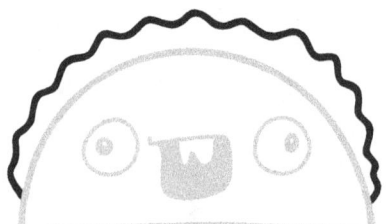

5.

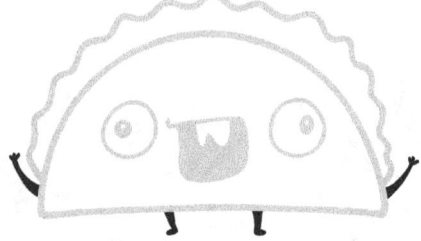

6.

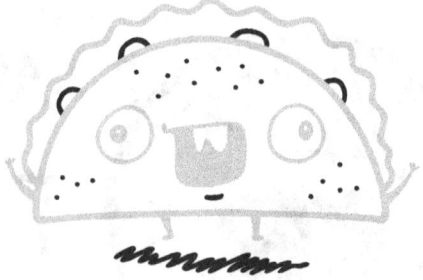

TACO 'BOUT
AWESOME!

MILEY CITRUS

1.

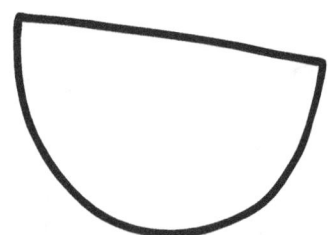

2.

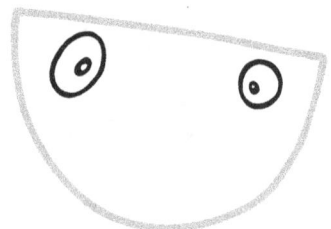

3.

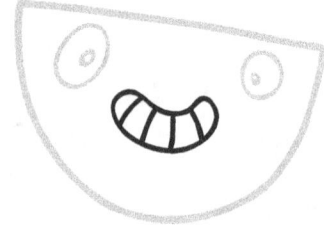

4.

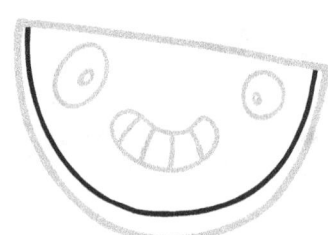

5.

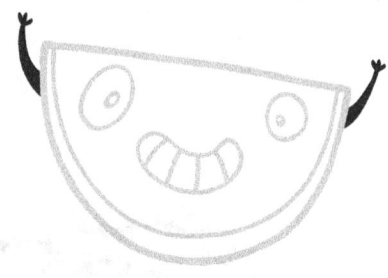

6.

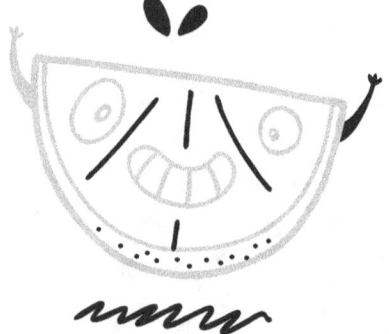

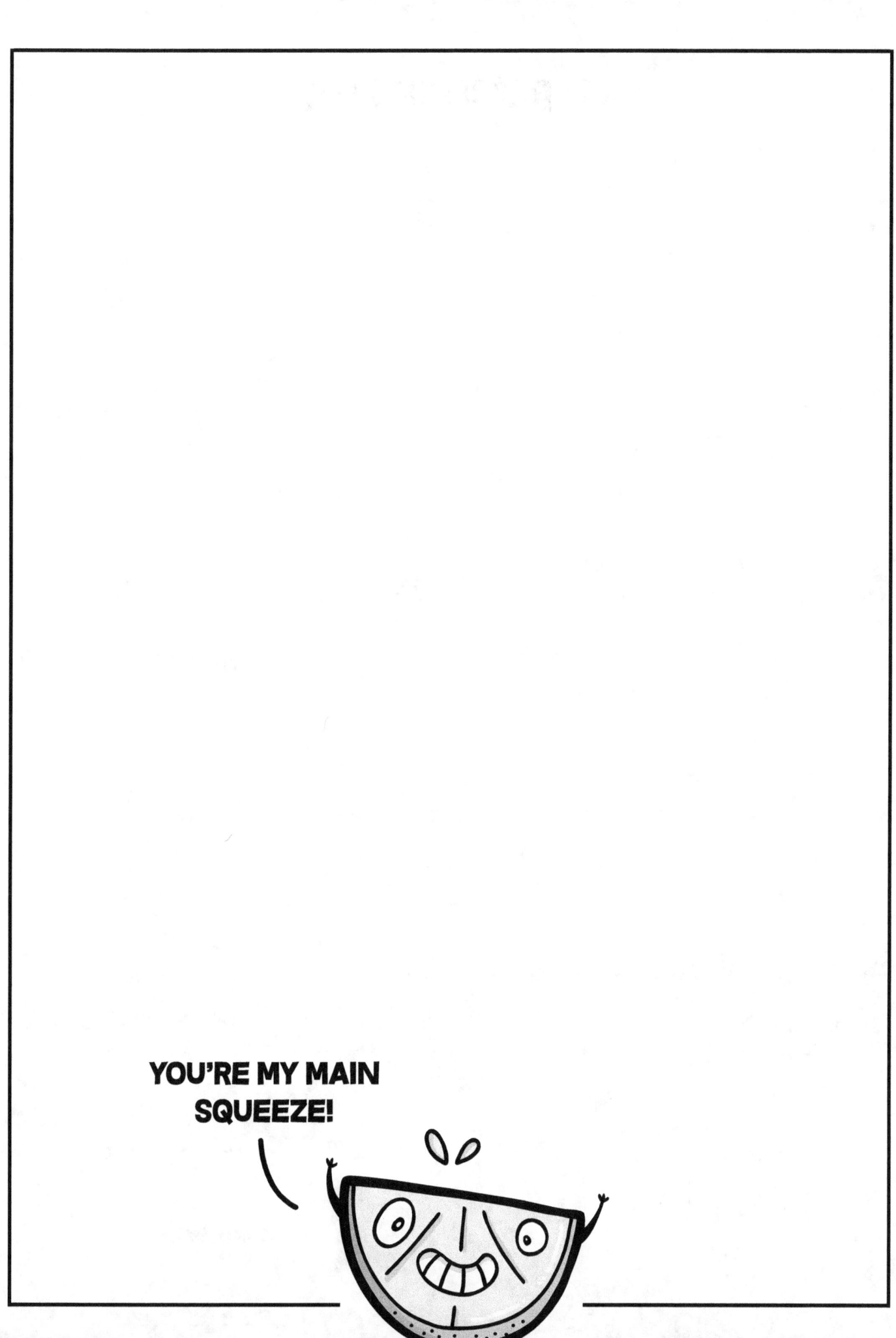

YOU'RE MY MAIN SQUEEZE!

HARDCORE PHIL

1.

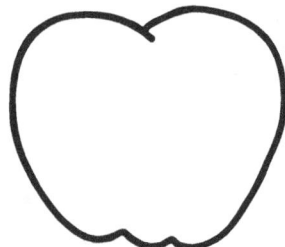

2.

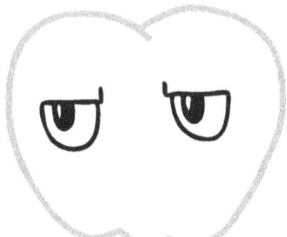

3.

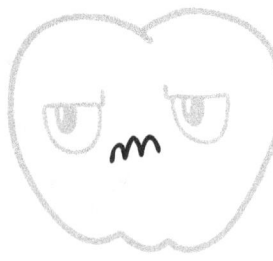

4.

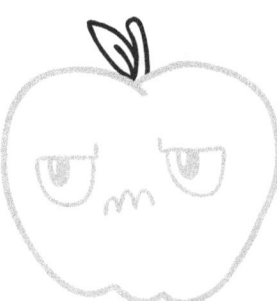

5.

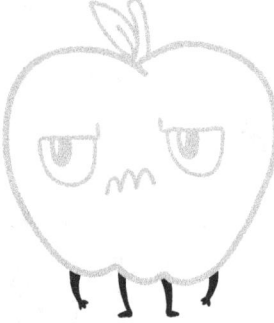

6.

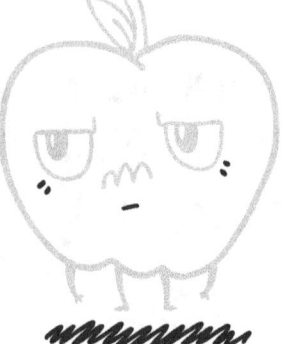

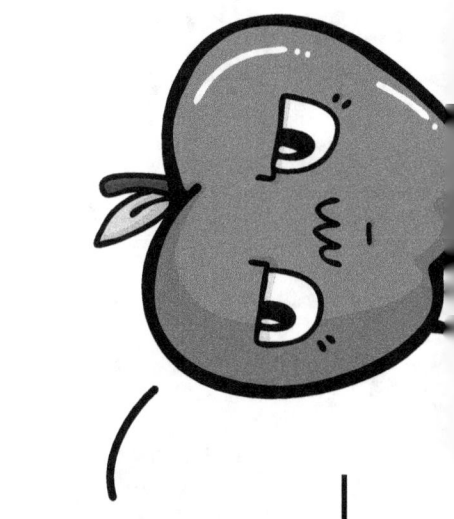

I'M TOUGH, NO
MATTER HOW
YOU SLICE IT.

PRICKLY KEANU

1.

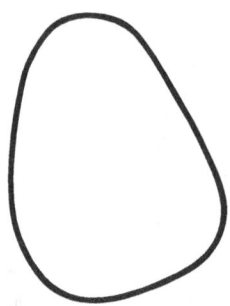

2.

3.

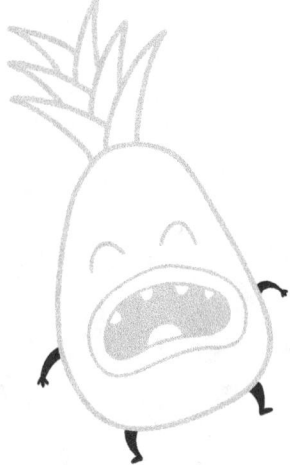

4.

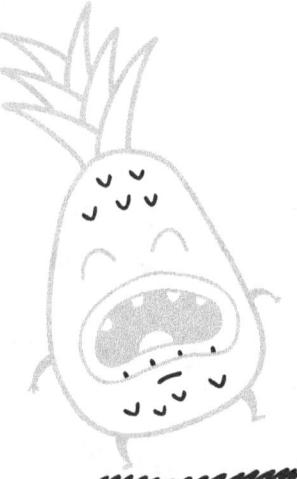

5.

6.

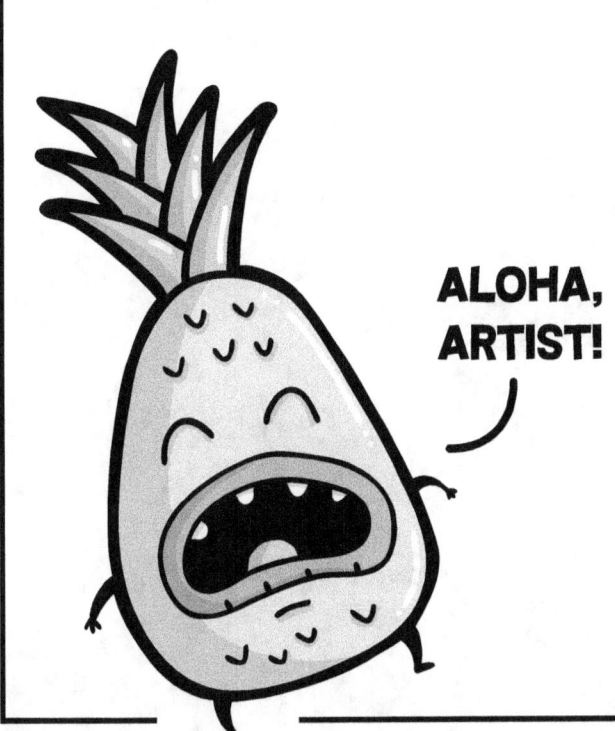

ALOHA,
ARTIST!

FRANK WURST

1.

2.

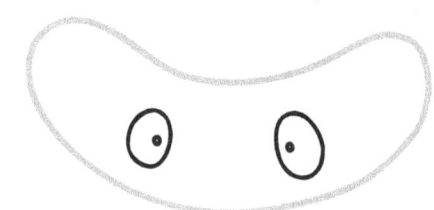

3.

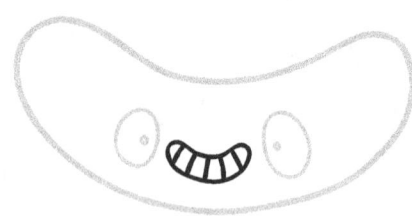

4.

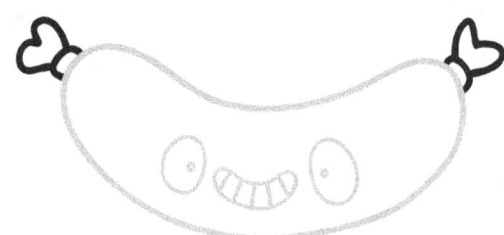

5.

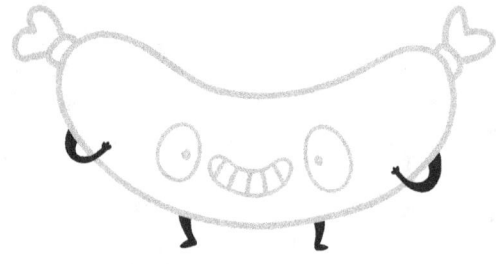

6.

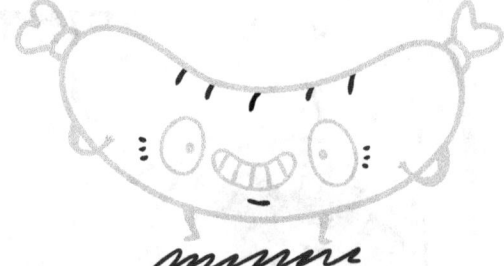

**HOT
DIGGITY DAWG!**

STEVIE ROOTS

1.

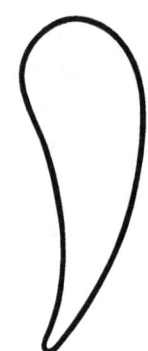

2.

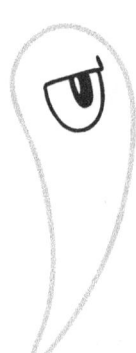

3.

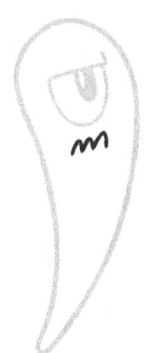

4.

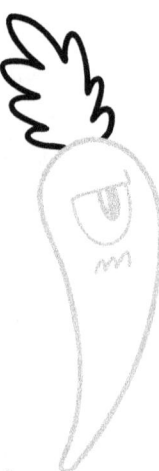

5.

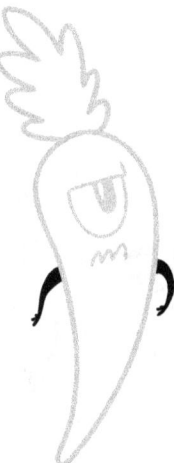

6.

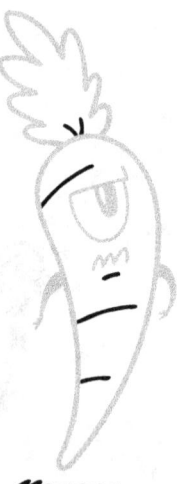

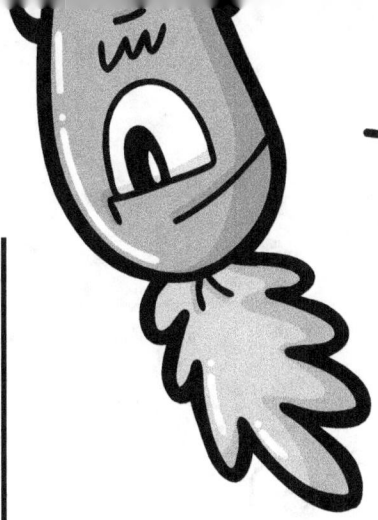

**I'M ROOTING
FOR YOU!**

VANILLA MELTS

1.

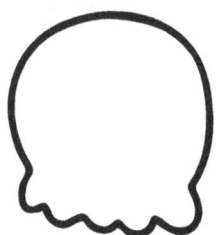

2.

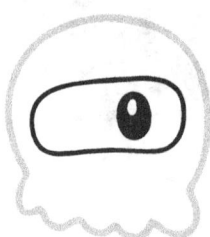

3.

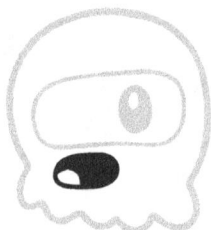

4.

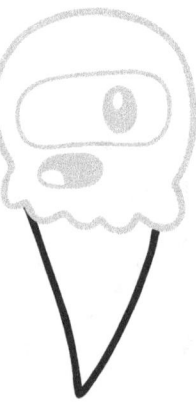

5.

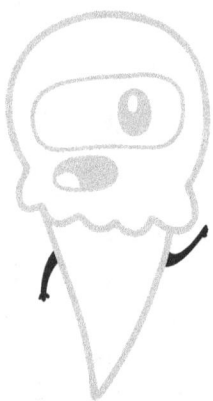

6.

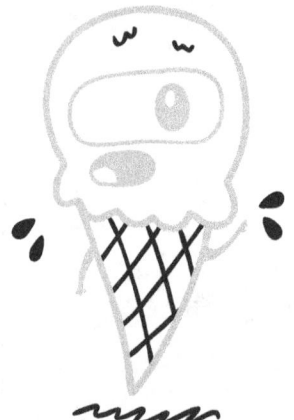

STUD MUFFIN

1.

2.

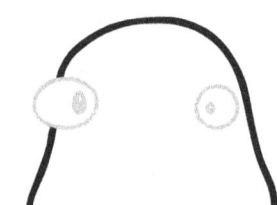

3.

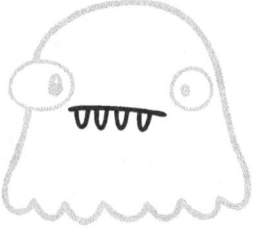

4.

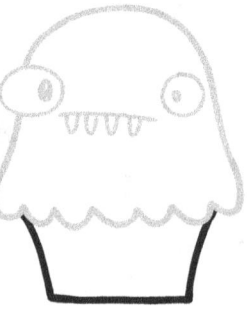

5.

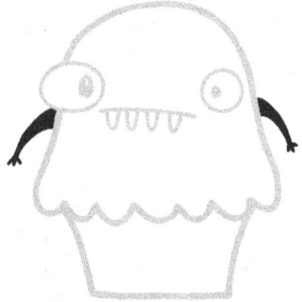

6.

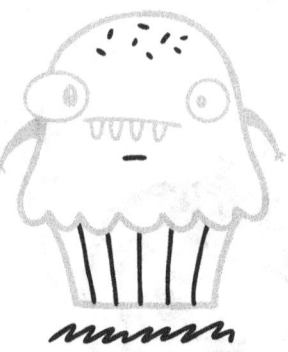

JUST LOOK
AT THESE
MUSCLES!

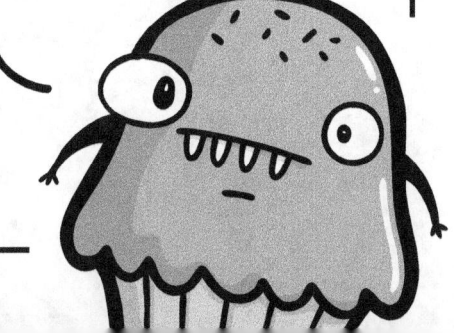

ROBERT MCBURGER

1.

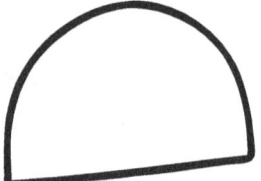

2.

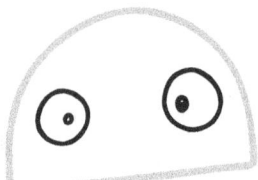

3.

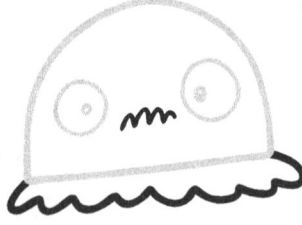

4.

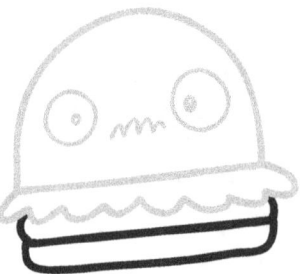

5.

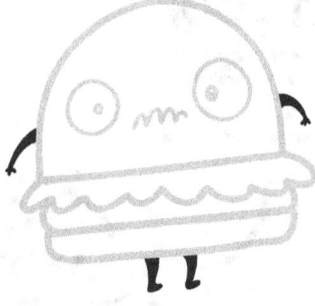

6.

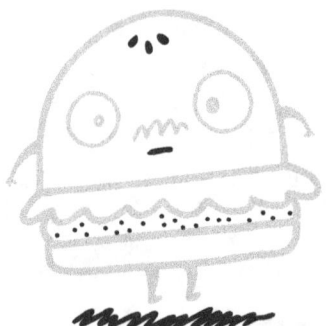

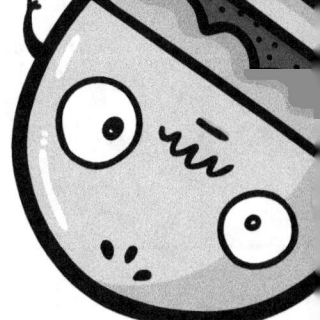

SLICE SLICE BABY

1.

2.

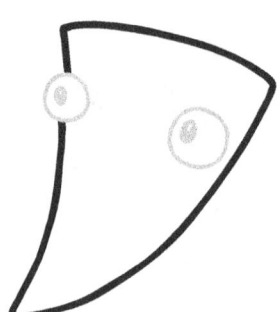

3.

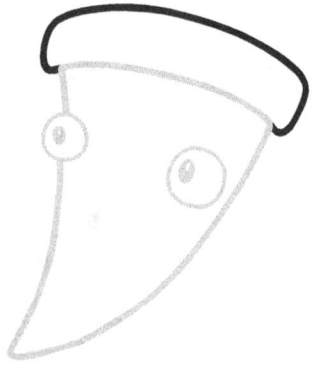

4.

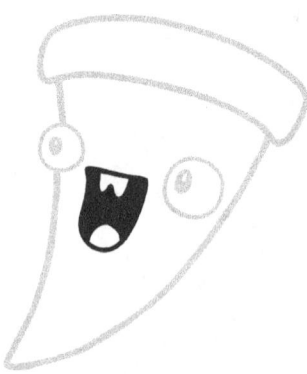

5.

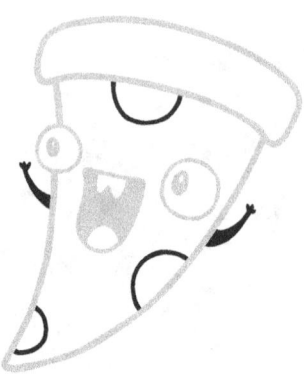

6.

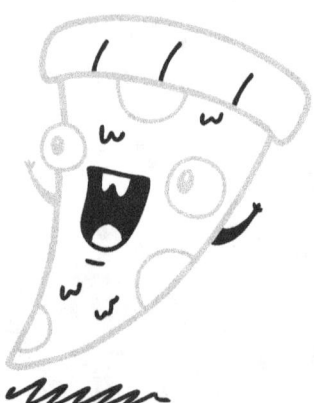

NOW THAT'S UPPER CRUST!

CHILLIN' FREDDY JONES

1.

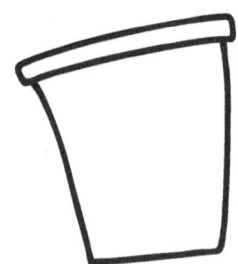

2.

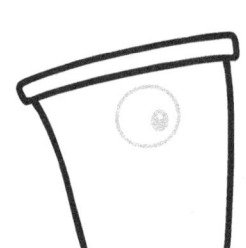

3.

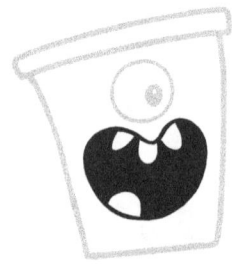

4.

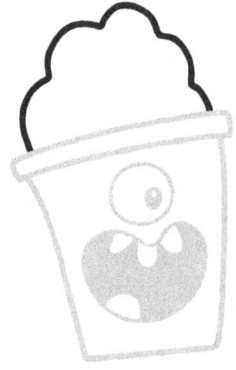

5.

6.

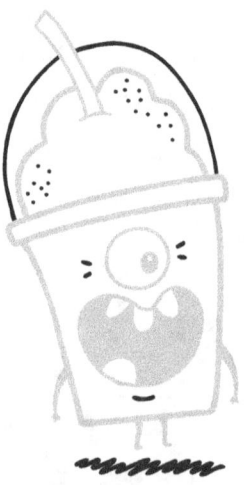

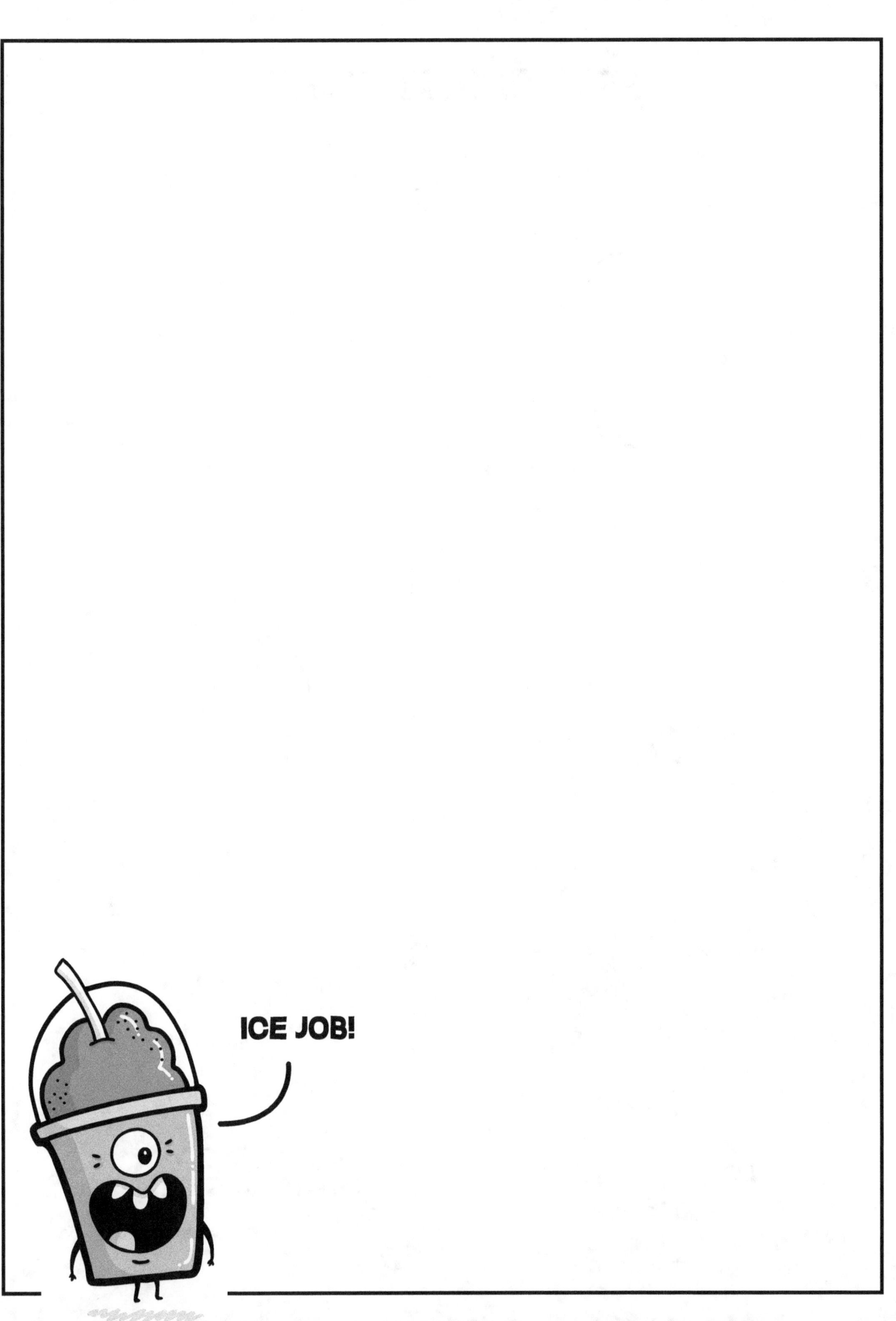

FRENCHIE LE TOAST

1.

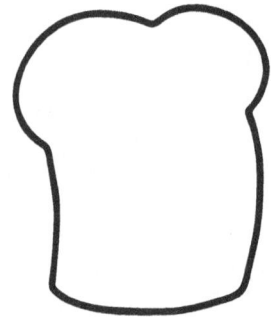

2.

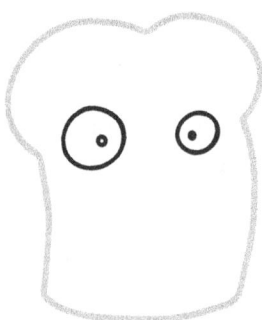

3.

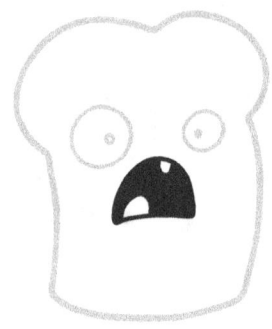

4.

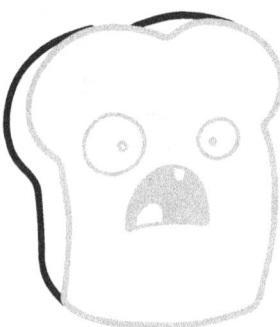

5.

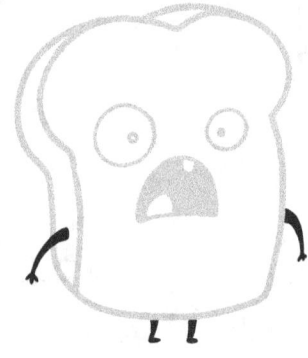

6.

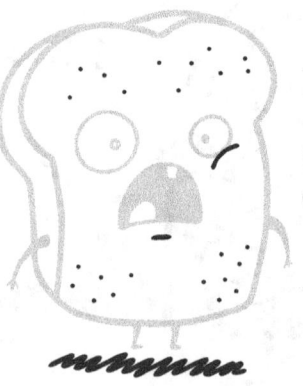

TRÈS BIEN!

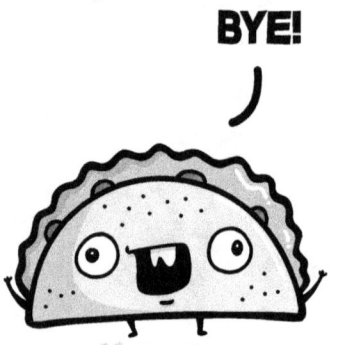